Sand Between Your Toes

A Watercolor Journey Through Santa Cruz County

Sally Bookman

Acknowledgments

I am extremely indebted to a number of people who have helped make this dream
become a reality. I feel so fortunate to have found the very best people.

It was by good fortune that I met Mike Miller of Prism Photographics, Inc.
He's best known for his photography and as the publisher of the Santa Cruz Calendar.
His enthusiasm and overriding insistence for quality and attention to detail
helped make this book possible in so many ways.

I also thank Prism's staff and associates,
Mark Woodhead, Scott Kennedy, Steve Phillips and Suzette McGinnis
for their combined efforts of production, scans,
final color proofs and copy editing.

Working with Mike, was our mutual friend, Cloyce Wall, Graphic Designer.
He did the design and layout of this book. Thank you Cloyce, you are indeed a master!

Most of all though, I have to thank my husband Lee for keeping the household
and our business going while I completed the sketches for this book.
I have been married to this wonderful man for thirty one years
and he has always been my greatest supporter.
Here's to the next thirty one years!

Copyright © 2002 by Sally Bookman: The Gallery
109 Capitola Avenue • Capitola, CA 95010
831-464-3838 • www.sallybookman.com

Printed in Singapore
Soft Bound Edition: ISBN 0-9723101-0-X • Hard Bound Edition: ISBN 0-9723101-1-8 • Hard Bound Signed Edition with Slipcase: ISBN 0-9723101-2-6

Introduction

The idea for this book first came to me about fifteen years ago and I suppose in one sense, you could say it has taken that long to complete. Over the past fifteen years I have been painting watercolors of many familiar scenes in Santa Cruz County.

Big Basin Redwoods

Henry Cowell Redwoods

Felton

Davenport

Wilder Ranch

The Forest of Nisene Marks

Soquel

Santa Cruz

Capitola

Aptos

La Selva Beach

Watsonville

During this time I have seen many familiar sights disappear. Most notably, of course, was the Cooper House on Pacific Avenue. Then there were numerous barns, water towers and quaint seaside cottages. It was the disappearance of these structures that added an extra impetus for me to publish this book, and not years from now "when I retire."

The idea of doing a sketch book, that is, pen and ink with watercolor washes, really began to take hold after I traveled with a fellow sketch artist to Venice, Italy, some years ago. From then on, whenever we went on a family vacation, I did little sketches which I colored from a small box of watercolor paints. I treasure those books even more than the photographs that were taken because not only can I recall the actual scenes, but the sounds, smells and temperature of the moment come flooding back and suddenly I am there.

What you will find in this little book are vignettes that have caught my attention and become my own personal special places. Believe me when I tell you I wanted to include dozens, maybe hundreds more little tidbits of Santa Cruz into this first book. I have included just a slice of what makes Santa Cruz County such an eccentrically fun, whimsical, beautiful and exciting place to live.

Sally Bookman

To my husband Lee.

Truly the wind beneath my sails.

— Sally

Sand Between Your Toes

Four Mile Beach got its name after someone claimed it was four miles
from the Santa Cruz Post Office. It's actually more than six miles from
the post office and now a part of Wilder Ranch State Park

Greyhound Rock off Coast Highway
south of Waddell Creek

Windsurfers can be seen up and down the
coast, but most frequently at Waddell Beach

Beach at Davenport

Catholic Church

The Davenport Jail, built in 1914,
was seldom used for anything but storage

This witch met with misfortune
one Halloween night along
Highway One near Davenport

The New Davenport Cash Store—
a restaurant and Bed & Breakfast

In her pink satin evening gown and feather boa this darling reigns over
the pumpkin patch during the harvest season just outside Davenport

North of Davenport, Scott Creek becomes part of an intricate estuary just before it reaches the sea

The 4500 acres of Wilder Ranch were once the main "rancho"
supplying the Santa Cruz Mission with beef, hides and tallow

Each winter Monarch butterflies return to the eucalyptus grove at Natural Bridges State Beach

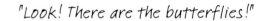

"Look! There are the butterflies!"

At the turn of the last century one of the natural bridges collapsed and another in 1980. Now, only one remains

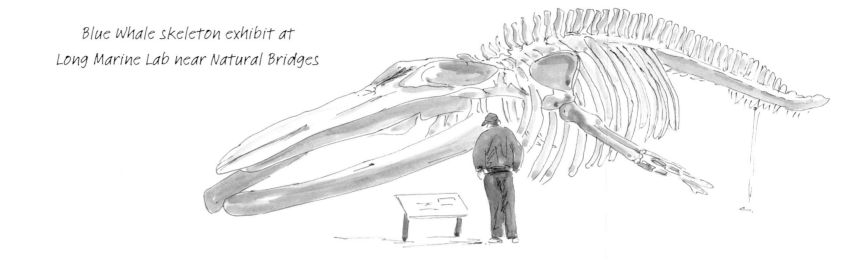

Blue Whale skeleton exhibit at
Long Marine Lab near Natural Bridges

Natural Bridges State Beach
from West Cliff Drive

Photogenic from every angle, West Cliff Drive is an attraction to all

The wide path along West Cliff Drive accommodates cyclists, skaters, strollers and sightseers who can enjoy views of sailboats, surfers and seals on one side and a variety of homes on the other

"The Castle" on Fair Avenue is actually a chapel or shrine. It was built in 1934 by the Kitchen Brothers, who were stone masons

A gentleman strolled into town one day and created these delicately balanced and ever-changing rock sculptures. They were a marvelous sight for months. Talent like this often appears and then disappears in Santa Cruz

A morning bike ride is often an invitation to stop
and watch the surfers along West Cliff Drive

Sea otters are a popular sight along
West Cliff Drive. They're frequently seen
using the kelp beds to steady themselves
for a meal of shellfish or just a nap

Known as "Its Beach,"
many enjoy one of the few places in Santa Cruz
where dogs are welcome to run without a leash

320 West Cliff Drive was built in 1876 by a
Methodist bishop and his wife. It was first called
"Epworth by the Sea" for the English birthplace of
John Wesley, founder of Methodism. Relating to its view
of the crashing surf, the name was later changed to
"The Breakers." The home has since been elegantly
restored and its name changed back to "The Epworth House"

Built in 1967, The Mark Abbott
Memorial Lighthouse on West Cliff Drive
is a surfing museum and a monument
to Chuck Abbott's son, who was lost
off this point while surfing

After jumping off Lighthouse Point for
a session of "six footers" at Steamer
Lane, a surfer returns on one of the
staircases along the point's cliffs

Looking out at the surfers in
Steamer Lane, the "Monument to Surfers" stands
as an eternal guardian at Indicator's Point

Cowell Beach and the old "Dream Inn" from West Cliff Drive

Stagnaro's on the wharf is a treat for all the senses

The wharf is a popular destination for a day of fishing.
It's often a family outing with the beach and
Boardwalk nearby

A sea gull checks out the visitors on the Santa Cruz Wharf, ready to claim any tidbit of food that might appear

How do these huge sea lions manage to get up onto the pile supports under the wharf? In the calm of night their barks can be heard for miles

This lazy guy never seems to leave his post on the pier

STAGNARO BROS.
RESTAURANT · WHOLESALE · RETAIL · SEAFOOD

6.95

There are few things better than fresh local
crab, a loaf of crusty sourdough
and a bottle of chardonnay

An old fishing dory preserved as an historical
reminder of the Italian fishing families
that helped found Santa Cruz

Caramel apples at Marini's
on the Wharf. Their candy is said to
be the best in the world!

A walk on the wharf reveals the front side of the Cocoanut Grove

The Boardwalk is the place to shake off your inhibitions with a ride on the Giant Dipper, eat some cotton candy, play SkeeBall, and ride the merry-go-round. It's a unique way to spend a summer afternoon at the only seaside amusement park left on the west coast

One of the many
marvelously painted images
on the carousel
at the Boardwalk

The famous and colorful hand-carved
carousel horses with its 342-piece
pipe organ has been delighting visitors
for generations. The U.S. Park Service
declared this graceful merry-go-round
and the Giant Dipper
National Historic Landmarks

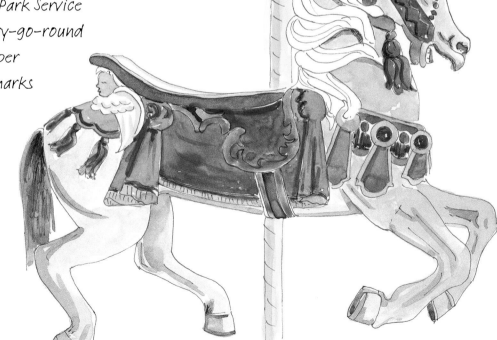

This very uniquely shaped house is at the ocean end of Pacific Avenue and looks like part of a ship. I wish I knew more about it because it is just so intriguing

Skateboarders try out the newly built temporary skatepark at the foot of the Wharf

This piece of public art sits at the entrance to the Wharf

Controversial River Street sign

At a time when classic movie theaters are closing around
the country, the historic Del Mar theater reopened in 2002.
In celebration it rescreened its original opening movie from
1936, "China Clipper," starring Pat O'Brien and Humphrey Bogart

For coffee lovers, the kiosks along Pacific Avenue are a
welcome addition. For the best "people-watching"
in Santa Cruz, downtown has no equal

Walnut Avenue Cafe.
I love their breakfasts!

Tucked along Pearl Alley, the facade of this bistro
lends a European old-world charm to downtown

"Meet you at the Nick."
Whether it be a current, classic or foreign film, The Nickelodeon
is a Santa Cruz favorite for avant-garde cinema

Santa Cruz City Hall was built in 1937
in the Spanish Colonial Revival Style

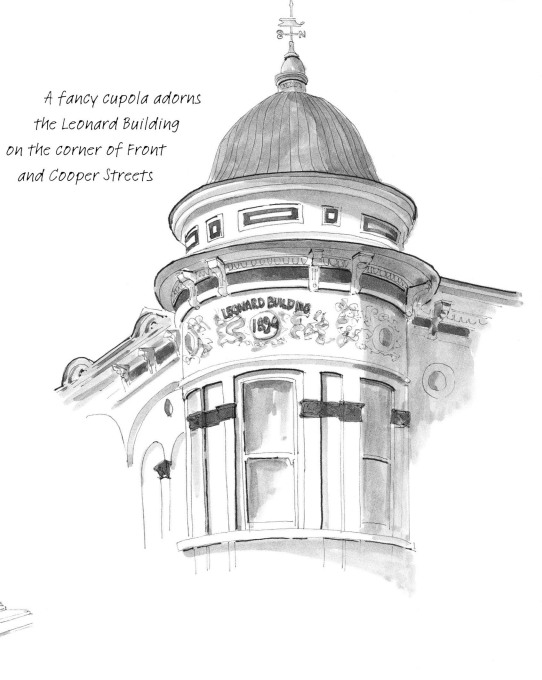

A fancy cupola adorns
the Leonard Building
on the corner of Front
and Cooper Streets

Across from the Leonard Building is the historic Octagon Building and is said to be shaped in the
form of a $50 octagonal gold piece that was minted in San Francisco in 1851. Completed in 1882
as a Hall of Records, it now serves as a gift shop for the Museum of Art and History

A memorial to those who lost their lives in the earthquake of October, 1989 is located on Pacific Avenue next to the site of the once historic Cooper House

The Santa Cruz Art and Wine Festival is an annual May event

Pacific Avenue, a good place to read a book and whittle away the hours

The Town Clock at the head of Pacific Garden Mall resided atop the I.O.O.F. building until 1964. It was reconstructed in 1976 as part of the city's involvement in America's Bicentennial

Julio Morgani, accordionist par excellence, dressed here as the "Transparent Man." Julio, whose real name is Frank Lima, is a retired stockbroker and now delights in creating incredible costumes for his street performances. "I am an American of Portuguese descent, pretending to be an Italian, playing French songs," he says

Tourists, students, residents (and even those with no residence) enjoy the ambience of Pacific Avenue

The Cinema 9 movie theater in downtown Santa Cruz has given back to Pacific Avenue the vitality and energy that was lost after the 1989 earthquake

A downtown flower kiosk is a visual delight

Elvis is alive and well in Santa Cruz – three times over!
These are participants at First Night, Santa Cruz

New Year's Eve Parade at First Night

Tom Scribner used to play his saw along the old Pacific Garden Mall.
A statue now commemorates this fabled lumberjack
and his musical talents along the new downtown

Lincoln Street near downtown is one of many side
streets lined with old Victorian homes

This Queen Anne mansion on Beach Hill is just one of many local homes with a story to tell. In 1891 Major McLaughlin built this 22-room mansion. Sparing no cost he included some extraordinary stained glass pieces. Later faced with financial ruin, he shot and killed his stepdaughter Agnes as she lay sleeping, then took his own life with a fatal dose of poison

The "Painted Ladies" of Santa Cruz are an enchanting study in ornamental excess. This one is on Walnut Avenue in Santa Cruz

The doors of this Gothic Revival house at
411 Cedar reminds me of the many buildings
seen in the Gold Country

Another delightful turn-of-the-century home
on Walnut Avenue in Santa Cruz

Calvary Episcopal Church on Center Street
has been acclaimed an "architectural jewel."
This wood Victorian Gothic Revival
building was built in 1864

The "Termite Car" is one of many rolling sculptures

Elegant homes, many built around
the 1880's, line Walnut Avenue

This elegant piece of architecture
adorns a home that faces Mission Plaza

Stately homes on Mission Hill

The Babbling Brook Inn is named after the natural sounds of
a waterfall from the creek that flows through the premises.
A portion of the inn is an original log cabin built in 1909 but is
now covered by wood shingles. The water wheel is a replica and
remembrance of a larger wheel that once used the creek's
force to power a tannery at this same site in the late 1800's

A weather vane on an
Ocean View Avenue roof.
Grand old victorian homes sit on deep lots
beneath old oaks along this street

A darling home dressed up in English Primrose
Yellow, Moroccan Milkshake Pink and Napa Valley
Burgundy with a delicate Provence Sage trim,
on Walnut Avenue

The Adobe on School Street is the last
remaining adobe of its kind in California.
Completed in the 1790's it's a part
of the Santa Cruz Mission and once
housed local Indian families

Holy Cross Church on Mission Hill
with its new steeple.
It replaces the original one that was
damaged in the 1989 earthquake

Mission Plaza is the oldest public
park in the county

This unusual building was originally twice as long. In it were barrels to store processed lime before it was lowered through the floor onto wagons for shipment to San Francisco. Behind the Cooperage are the limekilns that were built in the mid 1800's and are now part of the UCSC campus

Piedmont Court on High Street was built in 1912 with 50 rooms at an estimated cost of $50,000. No expense was spared to create the mission revival apartment house. It was designed to be a fire-proof, modern, concrete structure with electricity, steam heat and hot & cold running water throughout. All this at a time when Santa Cruz residents still heated homes with wood fires, pumped water from wells and used latrines in their yards

Now empty reminders of another age, these cabins on Cowell Ranch, now UCSC, served as sleeping quarters for their workers

Actors from all over the country come to perform in
"Shakespeare Santa Cruz" at the UCSC Glen.
Surrounded by redwoods, the audience picnics
and enjoys fine performances in an unsurpassed setting

Shakespeare
Santa Cruz logo

Joseph Ribeiro has appeared in numerous
Shakespeare Santa Cruz productions as well
as starring in television and films
in his native South Africa.
With years of experience as an actor,
director, musician and coach, he is
currently an instructor in the Theatre Arts
Department at Cabrillo College.
He's shown here in the production of
"Gretel and Hansel" as Ivana B. Sweet, above,
and at left, as Carmen Monoxide

A covered bridge serves as the entrance
to Roaring Camp in Felton

This steam driven, narrow gauge train at
Roaring Camp takes visitors on a loop through
the magnificent redwoods. On summer days,
the camp's standard gauge train takes visitors
through the forest to the Boardwalk and back again

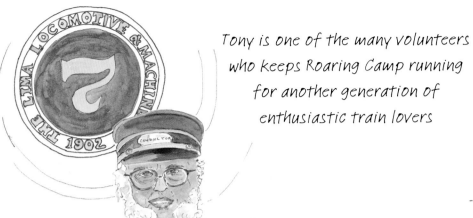

Tony is one of the many volunteers who keeps Roaring Camp running for another generation of enthusiastic train lovers

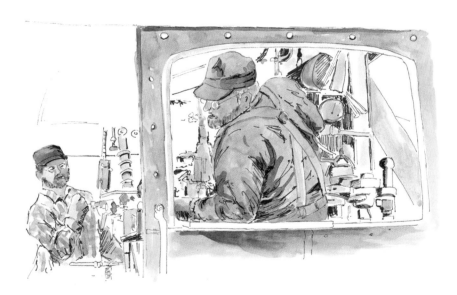

Lubing the steam train's wheels is only one of many tasks that the engineers perform. The name Roaring Camp came from Mexican authorities in the 1830's who found lumbermen in the area to be a noisy bunch

Once a thriving logging community center,
Boulder Creek takes pride in its tough independence

Roaring Camp General Store in Felton.

Need a bear? Cliff and Norma Short have
been carving wood animals at their shop
on Highway 9 in Felton for over thirty
years. Their granddaughter Margie joined
the family craft and specializes in carving
fur on the animals. Before settling down in
Felton, Cliff carved monsters for
the movie industry in Los Angeles

This fetching maiden beckons folks
to visit her wild and wacky
restaurant, Ciao Bella, in Ben Lomond

Henry Cowell Redwoods State Park in Felton
preserves many first growth redwoods

The pristine lake of Loch Lomond in the
mountains near Felton is stocked with trout.
Row boats here await the fishermen for a tranquil day on the lake

Sempervirens Falls in Big Basin
Redwoods State Park

A banana slug is a common
sight in the dark forest.
It's also the mascot of UCSC

Redwoods are found in many of our state parks.
Most are second growth, as the original primeval forests were
harvested to rebuild San Francisco after the 1906 earthquake

The vintners featured an old photo of the teacher's carriage in front of the school on their wine label

Dave and Ann Moulton now grow merlot and chardonnay grapes at their Burrell School Vineyard on Summit Road

Bear Creek Vineyard

Shopper's Corner—not just any old grocery store but a unique purveyor of gastronomic delight!

The 938-seat Rio Theater opened in Seabright in 1949. It is currently a venue for many musical events and benefit performances

I have never met a Santa Cruz Harley biker I didn't like!

The Seabright Brewery is a local favorite for its beer and "pub food"

The whale outside the Santa Cruz Natural History Museum in Seabright is waiting for some youngster to climb all over her!

The Harbor Master's house at the Santa Cruz Harbor

A peaceful setting along the Upper Harbor

Reflections of boats dance on the water

The new Walton Lighthouse

On summer evenings, the jetty at the harbor is a great place to watch the Wednesday night sailboat races

Enjoyed by locals and visitors alike, Aldo's is a favorite eatery known for its morning to afternoon menu of omelettes to burgers

"Are there any books on trains?"
Searching for books at the flea market

Sadly, Buckhart's Candies on East Cliff Drive
closed their doors in 2002

The Flea Market at the Skyview Drive-in Theater near Soquel
is the Santa Cruz version of E-Bay

The ducks, geese and pigeons at Twin Lake State Beach
look forward to their daily visits with the children

Over 14,000 participants run in the annual
Wharf to Wharf race held at the end of July

Parade of geese at Schwann's Lagoon. Cut off from the ebb
and tide of the ocean, it's now a fresh water lake

Local Woody

Pleasure Point

Clinging to the cliff on Pleasure Point,
this little blue building is said to
have been a lighthouse at one time

A memorial to lost surfer, Jay Moriarity, in Pleasure Point

Tattoos are pretty common in Santa Cruz.
These are the arms of my friend Cloyce who
helped put this book together

"Broken but United."
A Surfers' memorial to September 11, 2001

Capitola Beach — a family favorite for generations

Strolling along the banks of Soquel Creek is like a walk back in time. Little cottages, flowers running along rickety fences, ducks floating on the water and the warm sun filtering through overhanging trees

The familiar and colorful buildings of Venetian Court date back to 1923

Fishing off Capitola wharf provides a splendid view of Capitola Village

The old Windmill House on Riverview Drive was built in 1920 on the site of the Camp Capitola livery stables

The Capitola "Cats" set sail

Children in the Capitola Junior Lifeguards
get instruction on water safety, but mostly
enjoy their workouts under the summer sun

Wally's Swing World is a crowd favorite that performs
during the summer Twilight Concerts along the esplanade

Capitola Avenue, the main street in the village
is where my gallery can be found —
the little house on the left with the bench

The Community Garden in Capitola offers an opportunity for nearby apartment dwellers to grow their own vegetables and flowers

"Sand Between your Toes,"
playing at the beach

The Venetian Court is a beautiful profusion of pastel
colors on the beach. The court's European-flavor makes it
one of the most recognizable landmarks of Capitola

The sand castle building contest during the Begonia Festival.
A favorite event for contestants of all ages

Construction of a float requires many
volunteers and hours of time

Volunteers meet at Brown's Ranch
in Seaside the day before the
Capitola Begonia Festival
to gather hundreds of flowers

Each flower is carefully selected
and gently laid in a box

Imagination is given free reign

Held during the first weekend of September for over fifty years, this festival is always a fun event. Floats are decorated with begonias and pulled down Soquel Creek to the lagoon next to the beach

The Capitola Begonia parade, where floats really float

CAPITOLA
THEATER

View of Capitola Wharf and Village from Depot Hill

The Shadowbrook Restaurant overlooking Soquel Creek in Capitola
is accessible by a little red cable car or a foot path surrounded
by lush gardens and splashing fountains

Church of John the Baptist was built
around the 1890's on Depot Hill

The Six Sisters were designated an Historic District in 1987.
Photos dating back to 1910 show train tracks running in front
of these buildings bringing tourists to the Village

Rispin Mansion was built by Henry Allen Rispin, an oil millionaire who purchased enormous tracts of land in Capitola in the 1920's and later died penniless. The Poor Clare Nuns purchased the mansion in the 1940's and stayed 23 years. It now sits abandoned behind thick stucco walls and metal fencing awaiting its next occupants. Will it be an elegant bed & breakfast, a library or a community center? We shall have to wait and see

One of the county's very few remaining water towers. This one is on Prospect Avenue, in Capitola

Gayle's is Capitola's landmark bakery

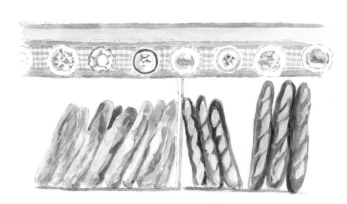

Baguettes line the bakery's wall

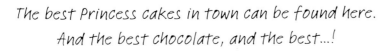

The best Princess cakes in town can be found here.
And the best chocolate, and the best...!

Founded in October of 1852, Soquel began as a logging town providing redwood to the growing city of San Francisco. Lumber was sent by ship from the pier at the end of Soquel Wharf Road

Driving down the hill into Soquel Village,
the view of the little white church
looks like it belongs in New England

The Farm in Soquel. Once a restaurant in an old farmhouse with shops and gardens, it was the scene of many banquets, weddings and casual dining events. Driving past the old house now reminds me of those happy times

Vineyards are scattered throughout
the mountains of Santa Cruz. This one
is located on Chardonnay Lane in Soquel

When it rains, the geese don yellow rain slickers;
on Easter they appear in bonnets and dresses;
and during football season...
well, you get the idea!

Casalegno's grocery store, at the corner of Laurel Glen and
Old San Jose Road, serves the mountain community
as a meeting place, advice center and deli

Norman Bei of Soquel began this train topiary in 1993.
Made entirely of various shrubs, such as camellias, privet,
ivy and juniper, it's an immaculately maintained 30' long floral sculpture

The drive along Park Avenue
from Capitola to New Brighton
State Beach provides
a lovely coastline
view through eucalyptus
trees that line its roadway

This old wooden boat is docked on a street
in Seacliff. I love the way nasturtiums
climb all over it in wild abandon

New Brighton State Beach

In the spring, poppies decorate this path that leads down to Seacliff State Beach in Aptos

Steel was a sparse commodity during World War One so the US Navy built three experimental concrete ships. The war ended by the time the ships were completed and they were never used. In 1929, the Palo Alto made its only voyage in tow from Oakland to Seacliff where it was remodeled as an entertainment ship. The endeavor went bust after two years, and the ship was stripped and abandoned. Wildlife are now its only guests as the relentless sea has finally made the deck unsafe for people

From this bluff in Seacliff you can look down into the area locally known as Aptos Beach Flats

The water of Monterey Bay rarely gets above 59 degrees. That's okay for some children and a quick dip for one brave daddy

Looking out over Rio del Mar towards Seacliff

Feeding sea gulls along the promenade at Seacliff State Beach

The beach and hillside at Rio Del Mar

This covered bridge leads into the quaint
log cabin shops of Redwood Village

The Forest of Nisene Marks State Park in Aptos
is a favorite area for runners and cyclists

Situated in Redwood Village is the Velvet Petal.
It's only one of many delightful florists
that are found throughout the county

The Bayview Hotel, established in 1878 and currently a Bed & Breakfast inn, was moved 100 feet to its present site in 1946

Aptos Village keeps an old-fashioned flavor with its wooden boardwalk

The 4th of July Parade in Aptos is
known as the "World's Shortest Parade."
Maybe it's named for the short distance it travels
since the number of participants has increased
significantly throughout the years.

This little girl and her dog proudly show their patriotism.

Face painting is a necessary part of the day's celebration

During the parade, Little Bo Beep found her Chihuahuas, I mean sheep

This lady sells her produce and flowers every
Saturday at the Aptos Farmer's Market

I've been purchasing narcissus from this
seller at the Farmer's Market for
so many years that I've lost count

Putting the finishing touches on a fruit tart in
the kitchen of The Farm Bakery

A labor of love, they are as beautiful
as they are delicious!
The Farm Restaurant closed,
but fortunately, its bakery lives on...

The arbor at La Selva Beach

Twice a day you can hear the rumble of the train as it travels between Davenport and Salinas. Here the tracks hug the coastline as it crosses the trestle in La Selva Beach

Springtime at Seascape Golf Course in Rio del Mar

This old packing shed, a common sight in this area, is on Pleasant Valley Road

If you drive south on Highway 1 you can't help
but notice this once grand home falling to ruin
among the Watsonville strawberry fields

Apples are one of many lucrative crops
grown in Santa Cruz County's rich soil

The current owner of Pleasant Valley School was a
student there for 7 years in the 1930's.
His grandfather, an emigrant from the Azores,
built this school in the late 1800's

Some wonderful examples of architecture
can be found along
Main Street in Watsonville

Look carefully and you
will see intricate motifs
on many buildings

This marvelous art deco style movie theater charged
customers 23¢ for general admission when
it opened as the California Theater in 1923.
It also offered a "high class" vaudeville performance
every Sunday. In 1931 it became The Fox Theater

One of the many ornate and
colorful buildings in Watsonville

One of several carvings
around the pavilion in Watsonville Plaza

In the center of town, Watsonville Plaza is adorned with a pavilion, a fountain and even a cannon.
The plaza is a daily gathering place for relaxing and discussing the day's activities.
It's also the scene for many colorful holiday events

The cannon's plaque says that it fired
the first salute to the news
when California was admitted to the Union

I was attracted to the expansive circular
veranda on this elegant home built in the late
1880's on East Beach Street in Watsonville

St. Patrick's Church, built by William Week in 1903,
was severely damaged in the 1989 earthquake.
It became a symbol of Watsonville's restoration efforts

This elaborately designed building on East Lake Avenue
is currently being used as a real estate office

Livestock and rodeo events are some of the many
activities to enjoy with family and friends at the
Santa Cruz County Fair in Watsonville every September

The best strawberries in the world come from Watsonville

Roadside stands pop up throughout the county
during strawberry season

Wholesale nurseries are among the many agricultural
endeavors found in the fertile Pajaro Valley

Brussel sprouts and artichokes love the fog
along the coast from Watsonville to Castroville

The End

But the journey continues...

References

"Watsonville: Memories that Linger," Vol. 2 Betty Lewis, Valley Publishers, 1980

"They Called it Home," Margaret Koch, Valley Publishers, 1974

"Santa Cruz County, Parade of the Past," Margaret Koch, 1973 Valley Publishers

"Soquel Landing to Capitola by the Sea," Sandy Lydon and Carolyn Swift,
California History Center, DeAnza College, 1978

My thanks to the following people: Toni Castro, Capitola Chamber of Commerce, for the use of Begonia Festival
and sand building contest photos taken by Joan Lengquist; June Smith of Santa Cruz Mountains Wine Growers
Association for Pam Stokes' photo of workers in the field; Steve DiBartolomeo for his photos of Shakespeare
Santa Cruz; Jeff Elmery for his photo of mist over a fall vineyard; Capitola Parks and Recreation for junior
lifeguard photos; James Morley for his photos of trains over the train trestle in La Selva Beach;
Rachel McKay of the Santa Cruz Museum of Art & History for historical information;
Pat Peterson and Carol Cuminale for their help with the text.

And Mike, thanks again for the "wraps," they're wonderful!